Comments on Oboido ⸱ ⸱⸱⸱⸱⸱ ⸱

"A significant voice from the African continent—a great poet."

Khaingha O'Okwemba,
author of *Smiles in Pathos and Other Poems*

"Oboido's poems are wrought irons, smelted and polished to smoothness, then left outside to dazzle under the sun. Here is a voice that's sure-footed, honest and has traveled the range of emotional landscapes."

Opal Palmer Adisa,
author of *4-headed Woman.*

"There's much to enjoy in these poems: spirited and engaged with the world, often rapt, packed with self-discovery and all the poems held together with an utterly charming and generous interest in people and places—it's very much about Oboido's encounters with the things of the world."

Chris Hamilton Emery,
Salt Publishing, UK

Wandering Feet on Pebbled Shores

Wandering Feet on Pebbled Shores

Godspower Oboido

LITERARY PRESS
LAMAR UNIVERSITY

ISBN: 978-1-942956-41-9
Library of Congress Control Number: 2017951266

Book design: Theresa Ener

Lamar University Literary Press
Beaumont, Texas

Acknowledgments

I appreciate the editors of *African Writer* and *The Indiana Voice Journal* for publishing some of the poems in this collection.

Preface

> We write of home—not with pen
> but with pain and hope and re-washed tears.

Godspower Oboido writes from various places across the globe in our new wandering existence. He speaks in the voice of the new young African poets in and out of the Africa diaspora, who, unlike our forefather poets writing from home, have learned to plant their feet and replant their umbilical cords in a new borderless ground.

In this volume, Oboido sings of and powerfully negotiates the Africa that is alive and strong alongside the new world, where "the traveler washes his migrant feet / with the wetness of dawn" and where "the road has mouth like a boa." This is a book filled with wisdom of a poet that fearlessly takes us by the hand into a world beyond the metaphor of home, opening us to new images that are African and yet not so African. Sometimes, in lyrical narrative, the poet juxtaposes western cities with African cities, challenging our image of Lagos, London, and New York, bringing us along his journey from the hills of Kisii into Nairobi, and then to the plains of Kitengela and back home to Nigeria, West Africa, because the poet is "bound by no birth cord."

This is a book about journey, about home, about loss of home, the leaving and the homecoming again and again. Here, Oboido says, "the Iroko tree has fallen / not suddenly / in the clearing of a blue dawn / but the king must journey alone on horseback."

Godspower Oboido's *Wandering Feet on Pebbled Shores* recalls memory of Gabriel Okara's "Piano and Drums." This is a powerful and universal rendering of poetry in the finest sense.

Patricia Jabbeh Wesley
Author of *Where the Road Turns* and *When the Wanderers Come Home*

Pennsylvania State University

CONTENTS

III.   BENEDICTION
The Road to Emmaus

IV.   EPILOGUE
Various Songs

For an adventurer I knew once,
Esther Oboido, mother and dear friend
of blessed memory:

to your triumph.

I.

TATTERED PATHS
Where the Harmattan Blows

Migrant Feet

"Give him time, just give him time,
he will crawl soon, the child will walk,"
Mother said when they mocked me the child,
tiny earthling, for clinging too long to the earth
when the other children had already bounced off to flight.

Time it may take but the stammerer
will pronounce his father's name someday.

So time it took and mother's little child
crawled and walked—here, there and everywhere—
befriending strangers with pockets full of tales
and a burden of unlived lives.
Of the road ahead no one told him though,
how it bends like a snake, like an old English lane
yet on and on it goes without end.
It is dusty too, this red dirt road, so the traveler
washes his migrant feet with the wetness of dawn.

The road has mouth like a boa. It is famished too.
You the traveler, bound by no birth cord,
continues wandering and meandering,
as if without destiny or course.
Purveyors of antiques on roadside
and the lives and virgin lights of new cities
are the comforts the heart relishes
as the traveler's migrant feet crosses
many troubled seas and pebbled shores, time-stamps
distances where the dream alone could not reach.

Tell the child, fearful of vespertide and mirages
which collude with retreating horizons
that the roads not travelled will remain quiet paths
like voices, buried as silences, in the sepulcher of narrow throats;
but the road trodden will reveal ancient legends and secrets
which no traveler tells but which everyone grow eager ears for.

Osun goddess

I have come to you, water woman,
as unbeliever and enquirer

to primordial waters of your myth told by
faithful mouths that venerate your legend.

At your feet greet the bulrushes, chaste
attendants of your aquatic aura,
water maids for your sacred worship.

True your waters course, tranquil your legend
yet so impure, river goddess,

impure are your tears turn rivers of brown grief.
O river goddess of the legendary transformation,

were you a dirty woman in your pre-aquatic life?
With your mystic mouth my enquiry give answer.

To you Osun goddess (whose absence greets my presence)
I come, enquirer from an ancient city lost in like myths.

Saratov Morning

A Monday morning, prosaic in its unfurling without
the familiar rituals of life.

Trees that are naked, stripped of leafy pride, stand
pensive like depressed war veterans

who, caught up in the ambush of winter, groan
tacitly in the passage of time,

longing, for a ceasefire of snowflakes dressing
their long arms still bearing late autumnal scars.

Green beards of mountains
lament in plumes of scented rituals

recounting the many struggles
it had witnessed on Russian soil.

Morning is swept off in liminal misery for noon
that comes with a wrapper

tied to its waist like a nagging Soviet wife,
to mock me in poetic justice,

and with its tongue the sun lashes me mildly,
in an unromantic caress.

Rain

And like wind-glassed tears, drops of
rain fall on our patch of earth
and write a poem of grief

on the alluvial muds of a chill winter day.
The sea is swell with watery tales to feed
the Norfolk broads.

Meanwhile under my blanket we cuddle
tightly for warmth—my loneliness and I—in
the coldness of an English winter.

In Overstrand, the local folks ease the pain of a
laborious day over pints at the White Horse.

At dawn the wordsmith reads some
Shakespeare and Akeh,
crafts a new poem that may never make the cut.

Through the window, vaguely, I peer
at the gravely despondent plants, arched in sorrow
from England's ceaseless drops of rain.

A prayer ascends for sunlight to fracture the clouds and
kiss the broken pride of wounded buds.
I listen to folk song, for so demand rainy days,

from a Dorset lad warming hearts in London
with broken chords and fine strings of poetry.
Rain shall dictate where I want to go next.

Saratov Days

Of my time in Saratov
rings lasting memories:

the pink-cheeked little girls,
befriending me without care,
on snow-dressed paths,

bent backs of old ladies
murmuring parabled words
to aged ears of their past,

the homeless dogs running
after dusty cars with rattling speed;

and the young men, high-
shouldered and lout,

who called me 'negro' with glee,
tearing several Negro skins

for not looking like theirs
or checking to see it was blood not mud

that flowed in our negro veins.
We wondered what flowed in theirs too:

blood or ice-cold vodka?
Fortnight after arrival without triumph

they sent, in two dispatches, severe punches
against my Black African face,

breaking nose but not soul.
Isn't it true that Russia is a big riddle?

Its past crawls from behind and stalks my being,
though seasons and seas away

the ruminant wayfarer is still not untouched.
I was a stranger there,

each day and every walk
into impudent glares from the city centre,

the malls, street corners and university blocks.
The traveler not left with much choice,

begins to long to run away
from the hostilities

in those pale faces, cold as the sea
and the biting Russian winter,

that reflected my otherness,
the new folks who greeted me

on Volga's embankment;
gambit to photograph without consent.

But Saratov, old city of merchants and miners,
is a bleeding poplar; dripping saps like sea,

like the river that Engels, city on opposite side, drinks.
How true indeed that Russia is a big riddle

not understood with head but heart
that never to Russia belonged, but kept on longing

for many things—like home, laughter and brown faces—
but the heart only grew further and fonder

of onion-shaped cathedrals and samovars,
of smiling babushkas; of Putin and Pushkin.

Crossroads

We're at crossroads here
this path where legs do not reach,

where journeys end and cultures clash,
it echoes loud in my heart.

I am haunted by our sharp differences
that we do not whisper.

You gaze east, I fix my eyes westward.
You reach for stars and the moon

with mystical intent—
what dragon are you again?

I reach for a higher light
shining from the Maker's chest.

I prayed to Him also—under the scrutiny of
your beautiful eyes, serpentine

as it is piercingly curious and arresting,
but your abracadabra, woman, I do not understand.

The Cacophony of Silence

All too suddenly came your silence,
like the moon's ghost, stalking pitch
darkness in the corridors of twilight.

I summon beams of naked stars,
pierce into my cavern,
this place of smothered dreams.

Angry clouds brood darkly
over my head,
a sign—or memorial—for our solitude.

Our waves now are ruled by silences
invoked by fear in place of intrepid dreams,
scattered—this haunting sense of solitude foretold.

Now here, I pray for sunlight
and thirst for all manner of Incandescence:
time for my own transfiguration

for left of my elation is pale fire,
nimble still to gut memories shared
and monochrome dreams insisting
on the dangling parables of a future unlived in.

The Journey

Abobaku, does the blue dawn worship
at your feet as you clump, irksomely
on that dusty road in pursuit of honour?

Maybe you are lost
in the labyrinth to find *Orun*,
in a forest of a thousand demons

where your ancestral assemblage,
wayfarers too of sort,
salute you on the roadside.

Abobaku for what are you gone?
Slave or prince, tell me of silver streams
uncurling at the mouth of Aye

that vomits you to Orun's intermediaries
like an honourable outcast.
Is it honour or ignominy that you pursue?

And at the finish line near Orun's gate
who claps, dances and prays for you?
Do you there find your king

or are you lost in finding?
Let it be known Abobaku
that all are free men in the afterlife.

Night at Dugbe

The sky maintains
the distance of God above our heads,

travelers all who watch
stars, like troubadours

in the sky, shoot whispers of light
into the neglect ears of darkness

foreshadows dawn
when the rock-throated mountains

with heads buried in the clouds
will offer their morning price of incense,

heavenward drifting
like a monk's guided prayer.

Three Cities

Lagos

Is like London
(but not how you had
heard it told as a child)
only
bereft

of
magic

and
imperial gloom.

Kitengela

Early sunset peel through
the film of indolent clouds
pierced by octopus-like rays
over vast Maasai land.

Cows, food laden
on both sides of the womb,
gallop home on low farms
as Maasai boys, some cattle owners,
also return from play.

Nairobi

These skylines with high rise
structures, erected
on resistant Mau-Mau blood,
haunt the spectral shadows

of colonial wazungu
that apportioned Nairobi's
whitewashed earth to themselves.
Kibera today is a postcard
of yesterday's apartheid.

Babushka

Head scarfed and
wrinkled old woman,
on tired feet she would walk
past me with a smile
and caress my coffee-coloured skin
with every grand-motherly affection.

"Marry one of our daughters,"
she'd say in Russian, with a laugh.
"Make babies here, mixed babies.
Make beautiful babies.
You're beautiful, this colour
of skin that you wear."

Her eyes like crystal stones
she'd continue stroking,
like the Virgin Mary, her son.
Ah babushka, gracious woman that lived
on a homestead near the great river.
O Babushka, old Russian woman
and friend of strangers in pursuit
of enlightenment on Russian soil.

Mami-wota Daughters

I wandered off to a place in Lekki,
a troubadour on happy feet tickled

by the white sands of Lagos, Fashola's
Lagos of great waters

where the ghosts of Benin war campers lurk
the shores of Eko.

Then a myriad of young girls
thronged past me wearing their

pink faces, strawberry-red lips—pouted like
shriveled crayfish—false eyelashes

and straight artificial hair
imported from Brazil.

I wondered, like the son of a pious man, if
these young Lagos girls knew

just how well they looked like
mami-wota daughters,

now land lovers dreading
to re-swim the Lagos waters.

Looku-Looku

(A poem in rotten English)

Looka that man wey nor get work
stand for newspaper table
nor be sake of say im wan buy
newspaper to read the plenty news
wey dem comot for di day.

But im just tanda there gidigba
dey looku-looku like Lukman
wetin all the newspapers carry as headlines.

But im nor buy, im nor read o
na just headlines im looku
but later im go come open mouth
begin talk plenty 'intellectual somtin'
"Fashola this, Oshiomole that"

im nor read o, im nor buy;
Na just headlines him looku
sotey sun com iyon im threadbare suit.
"Goodluck Jonathan na good man,
but Buhari na integrity man"
na so im shout well well.

"Arsenal na yeye club sef.
Na so-so sumo-small pikin dem sabi buy.
Chai! Mi broda Chelsea is on fire o.
Stamford bridge tanda gidigba
pass third Mainland Bridge.
No shaking, we dey kampe."

Na so so looku-looku my contri-pipolu sabi
di mata tire me as I sidon jeje for taxi.
E plenty, di tins wey woman pikin eyes see.

Conversations

"Listen more often to things rather than beings."
—from "Breaths" by Birago Diop

If the traveler, weary of market dins and roadside chatters,
plants his ears well in the ground he will hear
the footsteps of trees and the laughter of foliage greens
caressed by the cardinal sum of the prodigal wind,
grand commander of all things, bare before its sweeping sight.

"Hush," whispers the wind to the sea,
"open your watery ears and listen
to the melodious lullaby of my mouth
that your daughters may run true
into streamlined waters that wash legends true."

Rivers chant ballads under the muse of the wind,
streams swish hollow descants of hallelujahs
but no one truly interprets what this body of waters say
like no one hears the broken cries of saints
trapped in magnificent stained glasses.

Mountains, ageless custodians of the secrets of centuries,
hear several passing conversations but only whisper silences
for they are sworn to secrecy
until they are shred to concrete stones for urban motives.
They bury their rock-tight mouths in horizons,

in hallucinated clouds—transfigured by incandescent light—
that think of themselves as the Grand Canyon hanging
phlegmatic in the sky but how vain is this hallucination
of the clouds, growing no ears for all that pass above or
beneath—whether man, airplane or rain.

When you hear thunders roar from the backyard of the clouds,
know that they do not merely presage rainfall and lightening

but re-enact the ancient dispute in Heaven between Michael
and the *mimshack* cherub stripped of light and celestial estate.

"After all is said and done," boastfully says the sun, fiery eye of
Heaven, on whose mercy the elements are not consumed,
"nothing is new under my burning watch."

Addis Ababa

I come
as seed of Solomon

out of the savannah sprout
an egret on the grass highland.

Twist of the
famed visit.

Out the daughters of
Sheba bring, dark-

faced queens—
imprint of cave shade.

Sojourner with horn valve,
call, come to taste
wine of the face

not wisdom to test—twist
of the famed visit.

Out the maids of Sheba
bring, dark-faced queens
coloured by evening shade.

The journey ought here
to end at Bole
—this perch of metal birds

that missile men and goods
to clouds—

permeated with
incensed aroma from
St. George,

rock-hewn cathedral, in
Lalibela, consecrated:
Angelus in ascent.

And the star of Solomon departs
without fanfare or maid song.

And the star of Solomon departs on Sheba miles
in the sky—donkey distance away from fragrance
of *new flower* and maid *selamta*.

Eyes have seen
what ears have heard what eyes have read—

storied Abyssinia unspoiled
in one quick stop.

The Sand and Sea

I hear the slush call
of the sand and the sea.
In unison they call us,
pilgrims on foot, on migrant foot.

I see the waters, blue,
smashing the heads of rocks
but do not think my lover
that it's what flirts do.

They just laugh and dance for us darling.
They dance, the waters dance
for our thrill and to the rhythm of tides.
The sand and the sea, they call us.

Transit
In Amsterdam

Schiphol, this perch of fluttered lives,
is not the destination,

so, traveler do not unpack your bags yet
for all, like butterflies, are in transit.

This transient existence is but a shadow
of an inheritance, too profound

for my heart, grieved by loss,
travel fears and diverse cares,

to comprehend, so I will cling
to nothing but a promise hanging

assured beyond the clouds
like a white thicket immobile up in the sky.

Finding Atlantis

The soul, displaced and craving
sunshine, drifts and dreams of home.

The head wiggles like dog tail.
The wandering feet remembers the path home,

remembers the dance of virgins out in the
street. So heed I the call of the talking drum

of baroque tongue; soul in betrothal
I return for the countless time

in search of new dreams
and the boys who could only lean

on paper-kite dreams, needing
more ropes for flight.

They have reached the lagoon city for work I hear.
They will make it there, leave, thrive or die there.

I meet a land desolate, lights out
as are the people I once knew,

safe for a madman—eyes restless
like nocturnal fireflies through the dark

probing the sanity of the sleeping ancient city.
I have walked these roads many times before.

They are peeling now, shredding tars,
with memories and histories, ours.

Therefore, let me like the black
bird, totem of sankofa,

return to my back and find my past—
not this lost city devoid of memories

once shared and possessed.
Were nostalgia human,
I would meal its head like grass to Behemoth.

Forest Call

Tell my mother if you see her,
that I must answer the call of the forest green

for such was my night dream.
Tell her I hear the trees call

with the ears of a hunter.
Such was my night dream.

I hear many voices, the wailing of leaves
calling to betroth me, promiscuous land-lover

whose unfettered feet caress the heads
of distant lands, ever calling like Potiphar's wife.

I shall dance to the raucous shoot of forest bamboos.
I shall dance, bewitched,

to the call of the forest green
for such was my night dream.

To Christ the Redeemer

To you blessed Lord
I come, you who ever near yet at this
hour of my pursuit,
earnest as the passion of Gethsemane,
I do not meet here on this hill
where many migrant feet come to pilgrimage.

Your statue, blessed redeemer belittles me
your slave, (what use?) in this mumbling of
the wind—the offering of your breath

like the canticles of patriarch saints:
Moses, Elias, John of locust meat
and such saints after their kind.

Arms stretched wide, as was at Calvary,
you call, in your manner Lord,
the tourist, the lost, the found
and all sundry men to your breast, your rest.

Redeemer and Christ,
a sojourner come I to your feet without pure
nard or palm frond. Weary from the journey,
I thirst; will you bid me drink from your
well that I may thirst no more?

Ahead the journey is far
and continue I must. Continue I must O Lord. What
viaticum then offers my Lord to his slave?
This yoke, will you not from me take away?

Sao Paulo

To what do I compare you Sao Paulo,
city with muscle of steel, concrete heights
and hurried dreams?

Shall I compare you to the girl from Ipanema
who swings and sways so gently by?
You are laid out like fine poetry,
like a lyrical verse.

The River Tiete, quite dullish
with murk, these days,
splits you at the waist with unromantic meander.

Your landscapes, these hunched hills
are like alien guards over your shoulders, crouching.
And I, as wayfarer through Avenida Paulista,
collect stories with tourist eyes.

When upon your restlessness night shade falls,
your urban lights turn to gold dusts,
scattered under the eyes of God.

Hitting Kano by Road

Foreheads pinned
to the earth.

Like mantis,
men and boys on coal tar

fold like frogs anticipating leap;
facing Mecca in

religious prostrate.
Diversion signs read:

Slow down,
prayer in progress.

Now that personal devotion
has become public art

the traveler prays too,
with heart not mouth:

though I walk through
the valley of the shadow of death ...

Poem from the Diaspora—a Lament

With betrothal write we
of alien lands—now new homes
for travel-worn sojourners.

We write of home—not with pen
but with pain and hope and re-washed tears.

The most haunting verses
are the ones we try to stay away from,

the ones that keep us awake
like restless tarantulas weaving webbed cities.

Sometimes I think I am no poet by choice.
I am no poet by choice.

Nostalgia, I have come to figure out,
is a language itself foisted hard on me
—so I am without choice

to give wings to words, like caged butterflies,
protesting in the distances of my soul

the way an unborn child, clamouring for light and air,
protests in the immobile orbit of its mother's womb

with soft foot that will touch soon
the crinkled paths of men and beasts.

To give words flight is to retrace one's step
like Samuel Ajayi Crowther to a peopled bay.

To give words flight is to candy off the little children
so the adults too can play—but the words return

like the children that do not go away for long;
they come running back with new fancies or mischief.

There are pains and regrets—but also promise
—like blood spluttered on the corridors of verses
from a Diaspora that both dreads and dreams of home.

New York

Have the ghosts of Negro labourers,
auctioned at Wall Street, come to steal voices from
New York, city bereft of people with faces?
New York, where have you buried your silent faces?
Your lives are as fast as your feet, your feet
as fast as your subway—underground city of ghosts with long
plastic faces—lost in a rush without progress.

Things moving but immobile.
A kind of hurried life not fully lived.
New York, let the tears of broken stars be libations
over you: lamentations out of the depth of the void.
Wash in the deluge, city of steel and dream.

And now where are your smiles, New York? Where is your laughter?
Trapped in between the serrated gates of toothed mouths?
City of actors, but mostly wannabes—drudges at day
with lean portfolios and pockets full of dreams.

But when bills drain the pockets, the dreams, dwarfed
by Manhattan skyscrapers, die a natural death and dry up like saps.
New York, it is said of you as a concrete jungle where
dreams are made of but a dream soon becomes a reality
truer than the lyrics of a rap song.

O city of steel you are a great Broadway show with everyone
as players and spectators alike yet the silent masked faces take no cue.
New York has lost its voice too in the rush.
The silent voices take no cue. How deafening, this carnival of silence.
New York, where are your cries? Buried in the graveyard of the living
without voices or faces, without smiles or tears?

When I Meet You in Dallas

Like a riddle into a lair
the months between us have departed,
between us now is only a dream

out of our solitudes bloom.
When I meet you in Dallas,
our laughters, much fuller now,

will collide, become one and echo
louder than the Armageddon cries of
a million angels arched over earth.

Under your proud Southern skies our
bodies that produce animal heat will
reunite in a fervid hug.

I will come to you with a sense of humor
not lost in the void of seasons shriveled.

I will come to you, wanderer to the adventurer,
with a fardel of tales, a dossier of our lived lives,
shared in little England where our journeys,

now united, did not end with Shakespearean prophecy.
With a monocle now probe the future

for where this road leads, I already know.
Where this road leads I already know.

Now what elation does my coming bear?
Will there be a country band on the edge of town,

cowboys to uphold my cheer—
umpteen as my boyish dreams?

And why does coming to a place I have never
known suddenly feel like a homecoming?

It must be your heartbeat, big city girl, that
invokes my elation.

But when I depart, will I come away with a kiss
on my forehead or yellow banana for my brokenness?
Let this a sojourner's incarnate wish be.

II

THE MAGNIFICAT
Canticles for the Adventurers

Abi

Your name walks in sleepless corridors of my memory,
corners, where its footsteps hurtle fast like hurried waters.
Come Abi with your sunshine; the Southern glow
from your face. Come lady with the lantern in your smile,
unbroken,and let your breath stoke harmattan fire in me.

Abi, of the sweetest translucent life your sunlight burns
my eyes. Blind me, woman, with your flaming rays and
when you have altered my sight I will behold you with
the eye imprint of memory and heart.

Abi ...

Your name perches on my lips like the
lover's kiss, like a song gathering on the
syrinx of the nightingale. It smells like
sweet-scented jasmine, your name

is the melody of the hermit thrush, out in
the woods, swaying and dancing to the
music of the mistral that fan the tides like
God's wrath, tempestuous, troubling the
great northwesterly blues.
Bamboos that are nude and tall, leaning forward

like long-legged effigies, summon your name
with muted call. Do you not hear how they help
me call out your name, Abi?

A Poem of Parting

A memorial for Dani Curpas

Suddenly brother you departed
like a train, uncoupled, leaving us here
like scarlet pimpernels praying for sunlight.
Stand we then, as if on platform gaps in Bucharest,
watching the train lost from our sight
hoping it will return, hoping
stars will sail downward from Heaven.

I will not say good-bye here for I will see you again
o soldier; I will meet you in tomorrow's
winged dawn after the parting of twilight.
I will meet you at the golden gate
and in the sanctuary of light where minstrels,
the pursuivants of God, their silver sounds release.

I will meet you by that great tree
around which many children, bouncy with light,
play and flicker like dandelion clocks in timeless instant.
I'll meet you brother in that place spoken of
where saints, robed with immortality,
summon, with mouths of rolling thunder upon thunder,
men and kings wandering a furrowed earth with mortal gait.

I will meet you, at the end of the age
when at the feast of reunion
the morning stars, all like lilacs with tongues,
will shout for joy, proclaiming:
"Behold! Earth's children, sojourners all,
have come home" and your smile, once tender,
shall be like the sun, unbroken, in its strength.

I Will Write a Poem for You Someday

"But weave, weave the sunlight in your hair."
—T.S Elliot

Not a poem
about your blonde hair
attempting to rest with coyness
on your young shoulders
where your midsummer
sun rebound to Heaven
like shooting stars on
pilgrimage in the sky.

It will be no poem
about your sapphire blue eyes,
courier of your essence
and soul unscathed.

I want to write you
a simple poem, devoid
of the vainness of metaphor
yet behind my abstruse verses hide.

Then maybe you'll remember
the nights spent together
in the company of foreign friends,
watching random videos

on YouTube: of cats and commercials.
Poetry enthrall our hearts,
distant, yet not apart.
Then under parables of moonlight

let us speak of Lord Tennyson and
Okigbo, or Whitman and Nabokov,
Elliot or Pound.

So then alabaster girl,
I have led you to Siloam,
this place of water—and safe landing.
After such recondite knowledge,
what baptism?

A Portrait of You

You appeared
for the repeated time.

Not much had changed: your
hair still golden

and your smile carried
the warmth of the sun.

You laughed, gentle lady,
like the tender incantations

of hills on distant side.
To what do I owe this epiphany?

Gods ...

you called my name in half like you do
with the gentle halting voice of the wind,

paint me a portrait.

Then your dreamy eyes, that whisper to God,
twinkled like a displaced lone star

roaming about my sublunary space in search of
things unbeknownst to me.

May I grab my jacket please?
you asked, ever so politely.

We won't need it now or here,
protested I, man of mortal argument,

placing hands on your shoulders, cursive

like Colorado mountains,

and with my eyes consumed you like communion bread.
On a summer day, such as this, what is more beautiful?

An imagined picture of you dancing carefree
in the incandescent writhing of the sun, your hair

swaying and descending on your shoulders
like a herd of goat descending from Mount Gilead

or is it the radiance
that spreads abroad your tender skin?

Someday soon
I will paint a fitting portrait

of you on canvas
or keep on attempting to do so in verse.

Becoming Patricia Jabbeh Wesley

You must come from a line of strong black women,
from the line of Iyeeh, mother of her mother,
Iyeeh Gbelay Juway, and you must know how to say:
"I am Patricia Jabbeh Wesley," and learn to always say it again,
re-asserting an identity rooted deeply in sweat, in blood
and in tears of sometimes despair, but mostly joy.
You must be the fecund-hearted mother of many children,
a posterity like the stars that all shine and dance for her.

For the child that strays far from home you must learn to lash
with the tongue of correction, and when that child has shed a tear,
even a croc-like tear, you must recollect with an embrace
and a Grebo praise song for the prodigal from a heart merry.
And like Virginia Woolf, you must have no country;
Jabbeh's country is the world.
Jabbeh is the world laid out like many seas.
You must leave no one, no place or conversation
without a joke,a story from Medellin or Altoona.
Tell that joke too of the *wazobia* men.

There must be no man in your world—no half man
strolling with feminine gait and the borrowed waist of a woman;
or no man and a half, holding his woman by the waist, roughly—
loose man like a fish seller, in sweat smell drenched, in Monrovia.
And when you walk downtown Nairobi, you must wear
your bright multi-coloured West African lappa.

You must walk Jabbeh's rugged paths and swim
her murky waters, dodge the pebbled rain of bullets too.
Live her past—of struggles and war, and when you land in America
on tenderfoot, write, write Liberia, write Africa in America
with pain and difficulty. Bleed verse and memoir.

You must fight Jabbeh's fights too—not with assault rifles and
grenades. Battle-worn but not retreating, she fights on still.

Her enemies are not people, not even belligerent politicians,
no not people. She fights discrimination and injustice wherever they
show their hag-ugly heads. Horn to horn, tooth and nail she fights on.

You must pray too—for the feet of the children that come and go, bless.
Pray, pray, pray for your heart too—growing delicate from this coming
and going of yesterday's children, wanderers now, in pursuit of destiny
and a storied life of their own. The world is their theatre of dreams.

When you have learnt all these, you have learnt well
that no one becomes Patricia Jabbeh Wesley except she who, of herself,
says with the mouths of the ancestors: "I am Patricia Jabbeh Wesley."

Two Canzones for Christopher Okigbo (1932–1967)

I. *Ogbanje*

"Hurry on down, hurry on down,
earth-worn sojourner,"

cried they from the other side
where with nebulous eyes
the universe is but a parable
and a pained conundrum.

"Hurry on down, child of earth,
come claim a place among us
ancestors who walk the stairs of stars."

Hero-poet or spirit child,
priest of sacred letters
and the ink-sprayed shrine,

stoker of the fire dreamed of,
what led you, Ogbanje,

to write with the urgency of blood and ink;
was it for the love of word?

To love,
for God—or the reincarnate mother?

To war,
for the love of the gun, justice or tribe?

To die,
for the birth of a vista republic
that did not see the light of the rising sun?

II. *The drum's lament*

The spirit of the sojourner,
sole listener to the drum's dirge,

is summoned hurriedly
by cowhide cry of white light.
Spirit rising: lyric of the tide in ascent.

The raging tide approaches,
a gathering war draws near,
a gathering fear grows.

*"The child in me trembles before the high shelf
on the wall,*

*the man in me shrinks before the narrow neck of a
calabash."*

The trembling gong loses its throat to the drum,
the drum loses its beats, tonalities that prophesy war, to
gunshots that know too well the ethnicity of skin.

The curtain falls on tremulous eye that loses its dream,
the dream loses its dawn, the dawn its hope of a rising sun.

An anthology dies ambushed at a junction, open-paged.
Open let it stay till the funeral night of the sun and the moon.

Abstract Girl

Adorn your neck with coral beads
and come, triumphant,

through the mist of a lavender dawn
into my chamber, this place of words.

Break your eggshell
let me see you as you are,

woman crowned with garland,
while they try to redefine

beauty on runways in Paris
or set new standards

in London and New York
I will the abstract girl

admire, speak of you as beautiful
with lips of contrition that have told

no unpleasant tale of you abroad.
The world does not know our story,

cannot interpret our laughter,
split in two, in an hourglass.

An Abstract Dream

In my dream,
fragments out of an abstraction,
I see you, abstract woman,
again, crowned with garland,
picking flowers and things
in my field.

In my dream, I see you baking
bread after supper, becoming
Eve, mother of all living.

I dream of Christmases
with you, the kids watching
mummy kissing Santa Claus.

I dream of many things, simple
things like laughter and tears,
allies both over small joys.

I am a man of simple dreams
(you already know)
weaving fragmented pieces
like mosaic in simple verses
such as these.

But some dreams I know,
have dreamed, never become true
and when you probe the dream of the cat,

it is always of mice; so maybe my
dream, this abstract dream, is merely a
product of a bard's wishful imagination.

Passage
Elegy for Claudine

And once again
time steps deep into time; a procession in silence.
Hear now, o watchers, these indignant beats
from our lowering drums with broken ego.

To our smothered cries give ear.
Now we, here on this shore,
stare as if through a glass, dimly,

your darling oblong face floating away in the wind
but no memory of you shall become a mirage.

We know you depart to a dance
of fire with absent souls weaving lights
but Claudine offer us, only once more,

a whisper to break this mounting grief
& until the moon returns to dance
in your eyes again, this poem will be stillborn.

When I Think of You

I think of cows plodding
through Northampton fields to your thrill.

I think of words said
with the lips of thought but not as compliments.

I think of you as a pellucid stream,
running true, and running through us all.

I hear your laughter
breaking iron bars and crucibles.

I think of your radiant smile with daily manifestations
like moonlight adrift on sea waters cradled by twilight.

I think of rugged boots and old books
with you lost in the legends of centuries.

I think upon your freedom
how lost you are in the place where you are found,

how your soul without care dances in light
and your tongue a plea upon gratitude employs:

"Bind my heart ... Messiah, bind my incarnate heart."
I think of babies, you like one,

acknowledging no fear and loving courageously;
your love having neither shoulder nor burden.

Old Romance

turn on the radio
let us play something old

        &

country—hip hop is for children. so turn on the
radio

        & let's listen to
a small town
        southern man's
ain't no trucks in texas.

let us walk—& talk

        & pray—when the sun goes down on a
sunday afternoon,

        upon a verdant country lane leading to a
        stone shack with lichened patios.

let us laugh and dance, dream around
small fires

        like two marooned on a
caribbean island.

we may go to a place of daffodils. let us
acknowledge the world as a stage.

        you can be juliet, & i'll be
        romeo

o let us, two amateur thespians, stage this
           play

without reason, rhyme

   or spectators.

come away from the world,

from cannonade of sharp tongues & assertive
     glares

that do not caress but reflect human colour.

   let us just be us. just us
for all else are naught that exists.

     an

old song gathers in my mouth, lend your
ears at the distance of a whisper:

"there is fire on the mountain, run,
     run,
       run."

let us run quickly; take my hands then,

   woman so beautiful, and on Icarus wings

fly away, like lovers to a place spoken of in
   fantasies,
harbinger of the ilk dream—

   still of such uncommon places. let's go sloth-
hunting
        &

  people watching, conjuring up meanings
  from their storied lives, like folded maps,
  &

imprisoned laughters.
let's watch clouds
           when they turn grey,

            heavy with rain,
& roam

            bereaved in heaven
or let us cast spells on indolent

                      rains, laugh at how
the thirsty
   but flamboyant rainbow

                 bends with faithfulness & season

          to drink from the waist of placid
                     waters
&
   if ever

you go hungry
i'll feed you with endless verses

            like how your eyes
            are like a
         cove of doves,

                       that
go foraging for white kites
above our heads or

how your hair, when
         done two in corn
         rolls, recalls to
         mind golden
         fields of barley.

man with old hands of clay let me
    mould my verses for you.

III

BENEDICTION
The Road to Emmaus

Longing

I long for a place unknown
and suspended in the sky
where the clouds hiss down mists
and spit cold rains
on a brown dusty earth.

I long for a place
no one's ever reached or read of.
A place where the sea whispers
its azure melodies
and I am the sole listener.

I long for a poem,
a kind of soothing verse, broken.

I long for a song, a different song,
a song in silence from saintly lips
of God's winged messengers.

I long to saunter on migrant feet
to Emmaus, in pursuit
of the Nazarene's Ghost.

Lost Moments

Outside the Houses of Parliament
stand half-naked light bulbs brooding in thick mist.
Now they come flashing past the eyes of my memories
while Kremlin's shadow here belittles me daily.

Amelia was a child I met and loved.
Beatrix was another, tender and beloved.
Oghenereke—child of my sister's womb
I have loved from birth, that moment
when breast milk first touched his eyes,
and they opened like flowers.

I was a child once, tender and beloved too un-grown
from the memories of my childhood
like nights listening to father's survival
tales of that uncivil war, told to the accompaniment
of the *tum-tum* beats of rain drops upon our zinc roof.

On Cromer pier often came visiting an English sunrise,
golden and broadly spread over Norfolk cliffs
that wait patiently in time.
Its memory is ancient, gracious to us all.
The Parish Church, from where hallelujah bells rang,
still stands bare under a vast and distant skyline
separating man from God.

Waiting

Kitengela, I am waiting to escape
from the smell and spell of your dust
billowing in the swift exuberance of cyclones
and all kinds of rude winds without course.
I am waiting to escape to West Africa's
tropical savannahs where rainforest trees
with leafy ears collect loose gossips
from the lips of the wind expelled from Sahara
that hides in its sand dunes lost histories
and merchant stories of the Mahgreb and Timbuktu.

Nairobi, shoot me to your Heavens soon,
into your pensive clouds—altered by sunlight—
let me escape on boron-made wings
in the labyrinths of sky.

From Kisii to Kisumu I have not eaten
your cherished *ugali* and *sukuma wiki*
for I am waiting to escape
to the familiarity of *eba* and *eguisi* soup
prepared by a brother who wants me home soon,
a brother I will be leaving again soon
for the magic of London and an America
that beckons now with uncertain fingers.

The homecomings shadow my departures.

O Child, half child of the world that I am,
what troubles the itching bum at home
that it barely sits before the seminal
feet, betrothed to the world's ways,
is at the door again, going, coming and going
like Abiku betwixt two worlds?

I am waiting, on this Nairobi-bound Rembo *matatu*,
for the conductor that holds my change,
to meet with Khainga at Kenya Broadcasting Corporation.

I am waiting and hoping on one, mountains and seas away—
Lord knows who—for a sign like a Pharisee
that the man in me may enter a kind of rest.
The child in me waits for a mother that will never return
after several seasons that come and go.
So, then I must wait for the second epiphany
of the King Immaculate.

A New Dawn
Song of Abobaku

The old Iroko tree has fallen
—not suddenly—in the clearing of a blue dawn,
but the king must journey alone on horseback.

His messenger has lived enough to know
that palm wine tastes better when it has matured,
and it is best enjoyed with common folks under evening shade.

And now Abobaku has seen that the world is bigger
than tradition. The world has pleasures.
He has tasted of it and is bound to it—man of instincts,
till death, Abobaku's own death, shall crown him.

Ancestors, receive your own therefore,
o primeval gate-keepers of twilight,
receive your sole wayfarer; son and king in return home
clinging to Obatala's straightened rope—
umbilical of earth clasped to cosmic navel.

Aye, world known to us mortals, mortals to the world;
be summoned on this naming day as witness
for Abobaku has chosen a different name—*Abobaye*
may new mouths call as old eyes of tradition
go in search of his shadow—this unusual disappearing act.

O *Aye* like a harvest-ready farm
when the elephant, opulent creature of the jungle,
gallops through it or alien storms bring spoil,
I will have plenty left to gather for the season of famine.
Aye, mother of all that is seen and naked before you,
Clutch Abobaku to your sutured back: the cracks
of many migrations and excavations of your skin.
O mother earth, bind the living till morning time

for death lay out in the street, in wait
for the traveler that sets out without lamp or map.

Aye with your ears of sand and sea collect
these brittle cries of the fretful scapegoat
fleeing the tether of ancestors indifferent
to Abobaku's uncultured protestations.

Yekaterina

In my heart I see her,
Yekaterina with her matryoskas.

Over the teeming crowds
in Moscow and St. Petersburg
my mind peers at her.

My ears pluck the soothing call of her name.
Yekaterina, have you seen her,
the Russian girl? Fyodor's girl of several tales.

Look, she is the girl on the tram
sitting in a mannered posture,
eyes colliding with strangers.

Yekaterina, Russian girl of the dream poem,
the budding poem, but not the girl
of my dream, let it be known.

Yekaterina is Russia,
everything I know and remember of it.
In my heart, I see her.

I hear the soothing call of her name, she
who only exists in Russian fiction.

Girl of the Caucasus, picnicking
on mountain-top meadows
under the clearing of Russian sky.

The Preacher Man

Servant of Christ,
know you not that worse
than a goat in sheep's clothing
is a goat in shepherd's clothing?
So then why must you be my Christ?

Preacher man, I come to you
like repentant Peter to the cross,
but not like a sinner to the priest.
Before you I come, a black man
as you call me
but half of my skin is half the body
you call yours, preacher man.

I do not come to you as a sinner
but a suitor and you did not welcome
the stranger who found a crushed tulip
within your doors, needing
air and sunshine out in the open.

The Cathedral

Lay in ruinous waste in the country.
Much these days the vicar sips tea at his home.
Sometimes he proclaims God at the local pub.
The old maids no longer bicycle to communion
through the morning mist.

The cathedral bell lingers with a dirge,
a requiem not for the dead,
but the death of creed and country.

Next to the cathedral stands a new council funded building,
a place of a prayer too for migrants

who bring with them their gods and a minaret from Mecca.
While England keeps not with heritage,
a muezzin calls its immigrant faithful to prayer.

Peace

The dictator, clatterer of tongues,
clamours for peace
but who throws bombs in exchange for peace
and who mediates with drones?
They have a name for it. It is called 'Military intervention.'

"Peace to y'all my people,"
the singer writes under a nude picture on Instagram,
but what has peace to do with her nudity?
It is like a lone egret among vultures,
a clan of reeds in the armpit of baobabs.

To a Nobel Peace prize from Europe
for the peace that was dreamed of and hoped
for was the foreshadowing of
a spring of war, an Arab spring.

They had a name for that too with diplomatic tongues.
It was called 'regime change,'
or 'Operation dictators must go'
but who dictates who must go?

And then come some with AK47s and a
black flag for a new caliphate;
Religion must be only for our God the greatest,
they say. Say differently and get a fatwa.
Religion is peace they say, peace they say.

The Last Hide and Seek

When I turned my back
you turned to dust.

But come now, I urge you,
from the company of the woods

just come without your tantrums and fights
but my call tenderly heed.

Let your ears hearken
and come to seek, to find and find to keep.

Time tickles fast like lover's passion.
When I shall turn my back too

and set forth on foot, wandering
wherever the wind blows,

I will but turn to dust too.
Shadow and dust.

No More Shakespeare

After we said good-bye I grieved and weaved verses
that captured the moment's gloom that foreshadowed
the void her absence would bring.

"Oh stop," she told me, "*no more* Shakespeare."
Ah, to be or not to be. Lord what have I become
—Poet or sentimental fool?

She walked through security
to answer the sunny call of South America.
I returned to London's grey and gloom
and in misery attempted some more Shakespeare:
prosaic lines without sweet metaphor
like a bland English meal without spice.

IV

EPILOGUE
Various Songs

Bird Watching

You see that bird, hovering about
without sense or care between silences?
It is drunk with capricious air
for it thinks life,
that spans a scarce moment,
is one unending bird flight.
O foolish bird that hovers.

Biafra Tales

Come, you who have built huts
with words like me, to this
discourse, I implore
for us to tell new stories
that address the current,
the strong rushing current
washing the heads of Jos
plateaus to a summit
of pain and grief.

Speak of the current, of those
with amputated spirits and
bruised souls for whom the
sun does not shine.

Speak of the mystery bodies
floating on Anambra's brown
waters, the chopped bodies
that litter the streets
like paper cups.

Speak of war, of Jos and Maiduguri
new slaughter houses
where blood is earth's libation.
Speak, without hashtags,
of the missing Chibok girls,
our unnumbered suicidal daughters
whom we never bothered to bring back.

Speak of soldiers, of those
who die daily or imprisoned
in the Alcatraz of fear.

Of the current speak now
or tomorrow's children will speak of it
like today's Biafra tales.

Haunted

What praise will rise with dawn
whose light did not heal my heart,
orifice of a broken soul?

I will not praise the morning,
for my joy does not abound.

I am lost in myself. Alone and shut out.
Laptop and mobile phone my teddy bear
as I sink in my bed. Look at me friend as
I self-distraught, like a child.

See how I am broken
like a Vatican stained glass.

I was a Spartan, I was
Hercules, I was Achilles,
but your love has wounded my heel.

O conqueror,
do now with me as you wish
for I am your spoil of war.

In the Line of Duty

For flag and territory, we fight as enemies
in senseless wars. Hurrah! Hurrah!
Damascus shall be a town no longer,
oh, it shall be a ruinous heap.
Damascus! Damascus how I weep for you.
For when two elephants,
superpowers of the jungle, fight
it is the earth that gets hurt.
So the Generals and Ministers of whatever
sit elsewhere and discuss war with their emperors,
counting profits and listing interests.

What is noble or romantic in war and indeed death?
All who die as enemies in frontlines,
whichever side of the divide they fought,
rise like brothers in solidarity—over at the
other shore—not regarding flags nor
allegiances nor borders nor territories
but question why they went to war,
to inglorious deaths for lands that possess no memory.
Damnation can also be in the path of duty,
so once warned a wise poet,
and judgment is only a death away
but the oracle concerning Damascus
will be complete before my verses become a poem.

Poem

Make me no messenger.
Make me no mouthpiece of God,
prophet or town crier with gong
and mouth as a ready courier.

My trifle job is to give birth to butterflies,
wings to verses to fly.

Come now, o poem. Come out of the storehouse
of words and jump onto my page
like a skilled thespian upon a stage.

And through the narrow streets
of a bard's crinkled imagination

make no tryst with words craving
meanings and coded messages.

I plead, be nothing but a poem.
Simply that. Stick with my plan and be not swift
like the words of a young fool.

When you become a simple poem in a book,
in an anthology, perhaps, or recited by a reader,
I will go butterfly hunting
or wander freely like a careless, senseless bird.

The Axe

When it entered
the forest

the trees trembled
and said:

"look! the
handle is one of us."

Becoming Memory

To dust he has now returned,
upon the dark chest of the earth
his clumsy head now rests.
Does he watch his body sleep?
I wonder, or can he tell

of the split second in the alley of life and death
when in the hour of darkness
he surrendered up his soul
without the mouth of thunder whispering out to it?

Then we wept, not deluged like Christ in sorrow
but a mournful multitude gathered for his mother.
Some whaled and others cursed aloud:

'This is a taboo! It is a taboo!
Do not call the Reverend Father
in honour of his suicidal request
but his corpse give to the forest,"

that Silk Road where a thousand
secrets and ancestral demons meet.

He has become memory now
but nothing has changed nor will.

Fried plantain is still the first love of his countrymen.
No, the world wasn't supposed to end
at his departure, or did he suppose it would?
Coca-Cola still tastes the same way
yes, I still drink it if he could know.

Some things in life they say never change
like the dimples on Itohan's cheek
that do not grow dim with every smile

but flourish like blooming flowers.
Stan-boy still rejoices in carnal fantasies
but after all these years he gives us a good laugh
like the good old days of boyish dreams,
days when we skipped literature classes.

How a mournful gathering turned out to be a reunion.

"Ah look at you, you've changed much ..."
"Big girl, where do you live ... now ...?"
"Is that you, Stella-Maris ...?"
"Bard, you travel a thousand miles
across the sea these days ..."
"What has become of the tall ill-mannered girl
whose legs are like yam tubers, do you know ...?"
"So and so works in a bank now ..."
"It is so and so's wedding this Saturday ..."

Adam and Eve

Adam, from who I inherit this larynx
and loquaciousness, when he had
given names to all the animals
and no helpmate was found for him,

was caused to fall into a deep sleep
and when he woke up, he saw
a man made from his ribs,
called her a woman,
like he had so named the animals.

Loquacious man, he made broadcast
in Eden to self and subordinates:
"this is now bone of my bone,
and flesh of my flesh"

but what he forgot, man
with flesh made from dust,

is that his woman had seen him
first while he yet slept.

She offered neither move nor word
but stood gracious, trying
to make sense of the man and his world.

Dawn Breaks in Her Gaze

Waters converge
at the edge of her eyes
like the dew from Heaven
moisturizing earth at dawn
when it breaks from the grip of dusk.

Each new day begins
in her sultry gaze,
(where I was once baptized)
stronger than the smell
of her morning coffee.

When I am enraptured in her gaze,
like still waters
asleep in the arms of the ocean,
I become lost for words.

The Girl from University

Her patriotism was a little over the top.
Everything that was great to her was Russian.
"It's the best country in the world"
she'd say in English, her accent viscous like okra saps.
I would laugh and nod—not in agreement or disapproval
but would add in quick pace:

"The Americans say they have the greatest country."

"*Ameerica* is not great. *Ameerica* is rubbish country"
she'd reply, knowing I liked her Russia,
not particularly a place to be dark-skinned African.
I lived just near the spot where Yuri Gagarin landed
on his return journey from space.

It was a shrine of sort to patriots and tourists alike.
I first heard of Gagarin from my brothers,
who pronounced his name with more exuberance than needed.
I liked many things Russian,
like Gagarin, the poets and scientists of renown
whom my friend, the university girl, was fond of saying
"The best people only in Russia."

An evangelist of sort of other peoples and cultures,
I'd disagree politely—not crushing her patriot spirit.
Then one day, one fine afternoon at the mall, I asked her
"How is it that you use an American product?"
pointing to her silver iPad. I also added:
"America must be so rubbish that these Russian teens
hurry on to lunch at KFC," although there was probably
only one KFC in town.
She answered me in her finest manner.
"The chicken is not from Kentucky. Only the business is.
The chicken is homegrown; it is Russian,
Ruuuuuusian ... and that's why it tastes better here."
The poet died.

Superstition

Lagos woman.
She is staring into the void of space,
into the range of nothingness
in the market rush of Iyana-Ipaja.
Her emotions are as dead as *ogun*,
lifeless to her premonitions,
until the wind rises in insurrection;
dust as commandos of havoc.

Lagos woman takes off with speed,
running deranged through people, over goods.
The wind chases her. She stops for combat:
woman and wind in open combat
before my watching eyes.

"Back to sender, back to sender.
Over my dead body. You did not meet me, o wind,
return and tell them that you did not find me."
In ritual fortification, she orbits
her hand over her head, repeatedly,
like earth about the sun.

She curses the wind,
firing razor tongue in sporadic frenzy.
She swears. She prays.
But it isn't the wind she is at war with.
She is at war with self, poor woman, at war
with messengers of doom her lot find in everything.

If the dry wind blows suddenly and wildly
they say the gods have come with rage,
with wind and fire, girt about their phantom waists,
to walk the paths of men and to steal breath
from the land of the living.

Secret

I dread a thing—this betrothal to land,
not any land but homeland;
the luring of patriotism, sometimes a vanity.
There is this contrived charm of anthems,
spirited as they are injuriously misleading, sometimes ...
Rebellious Scots to crush ... sang some, elsewhere,
with passion and patriot spirit in a Kingdom United.

Yet to deposit thirty cowries to the bank of age,
I am already worn out, heart sunken,
like the hero patriots when they near their graves.

I dread a thing—a darkling tryst, portending
a brutal breakup, not with lover but land,
from a relationship ever so abusive—one that
was bound to fail from the beginning.

But we are pledged, are we not? Hands fastened
over breast we pledge, with dissonant voices,
To defend the labour of our heroes past ...

We pledge to flags, banners of our sovereignties.
What is sovereignty? What use, this currency
in the market of existence?

Are we to become tomorrow's leading voices
with cracked throats? Would we, mute from the
hour of birth, borrow voices from the wind?
The paths I negotiate and navigate, distal
from Achebe's lived world, are not set aglow
by Soyinka's hair, each strand an ode to history,
to the memory of land, traversed.
Will I be town crier without Okigbo's iron-bell?

Run and scatter across the globe as far and fast

as the wandering feet can go, duty will call us, still,
heirs all of a struggle that ends with heartbreak
when age folds up near the grave
like the tangled sleep of a sage.
But are we running away from war at home front—
or growing legs long enough to fight from the distance?

Author's Notes

25   *Abobaku*—the one who dies with the king in ancient Yoruba culture

28   *wazungu*—a bantu Swahili word for Europeans or any westerner

30   *Mami-wota*—also spelled as *Mami-water*: a mermaid or water spirit venerated by some in parts of Africa and the African Diaspora in the Caribbean

59   *Ogbanje*—children (believed, in Igbo custom, to be spirits that plague families with misfortune) who come and go by means of death and rebirth

75   *Abobaye*—the one who lives; the word is not a title

96   *ogun*—spirit or local god of iron, deified in Yoruba culture